D0676848

# Zen Reflections

Illustrated by André Sollier

Robert Allen

# Reflections

FRIEDMAN/FAIRFAX

Contents

Snapshots  9
   Introduction

Unlearning Zen  13
   Dumping the excess baggage

Zen doesn't bite  17
   Just dive in, there are no sharks

He ain't heavy, he's my Buddha  21
   What was Buddha like? Is he still relevant today?

Zen and cartography  25
   The importance of your mental maps

Chocolate in the here and now  29
   How to live in the present

I'm really stuck on you  33
   Talking about non-attachment

Pain is so close to pleasure  37
   Are our pleasures just another sort of pain?

Zen and positive thinking  41
   Is thinking positive such a good idea?

Tea time with Hitler  45
   Zen and evil people

The karma of cholesterol  49
    Reflections on the law of causation

Up to the elbows in Zen suds  53
    The pleasures of everyday chores

Everyone's a Buddha, baby!  57
    Can it *really* be true?

Zen and the art of mountaineering  61
    A surprise for the self-directed

Just who do you think you are?  65
    The importance of knowing yourself

Of mice and Zen  69
    Can we afford to be harmless?

Navel-gazing for beginners  73
    What is Zazen?

The unimportance of Zazen  77
    Sitting doing nothing

Buddhist fundamentalism  81
    To bow or not to bow?

Should we become incensed?  85
    Smells and bells

# Contents

Zen Inc.  89
Toward a modern Zen

My kind of Zen  93
Buddhist compassion versus kindness

So what about the Spanish inquisition?  97
Will Zen see me through the rough bits?

Monkey business  101
Zen and organized, established religion

People of the book  105
Buddhist scriptures

Whatever turns you on  109
Buddhism and tolerance

Buddha, can you spare a dime?  113
Why are there no Zen charities?

No sex please, we're Buddhists  117
Zen, buddhism, and sex

Surrender your ego (to mine!)  121
Letting go of yourself—carefully

Zen is what you are, not what you believe  125
How you live is more important than doctrine

Losing my religion   129
    How Zen drives out "religion"

Instant Zen (just add hot water)   133
    The quest for immediate spiritual gratification

Time, time, time   137
    The benefits of aging

What do we tell the children?   141
    Buddhism for the pre-teen set

I wanna live forever   145
    But would it be a good idea?

Born-again Zen   149
    The doctrine of rebirth

We're all going to Graceland   153
    Faith, works, and grace in Zen

Why are you telling me this?   157
    Self-help Zen

# Snapshots

## Introduction

I once worked with a distinguished scholar and expert on the Ancient Near East who contributed to a Bible atlas project. During one of our meetings I asked him what seemed to me (in my ignorance) a straightforward question about the limits of the Assyrian Empire at a particular date. He paused. He reflected. The grandfather clock ticked and the fire crackled in the grate. At last he pointed to the map and said, "Well, at the moment I think it was here, but I tend to change my mind every few months."

Writing about Zen, I know how he felt. The problem with Zen is that it's in a constant state of flux or, more accurately, *it* remains constant but the writer's understanding changes. This causes a lot of problems, both for the readers and the writer. The readers are looking for certainty, for somewhere they can set foot and feel that they are on firm ground. Zen doesn't provide that. You will never get to understand Zen the way you under-stand how to fix your computer, for example, or how to get from here to New Jersey. People try to grasp Zen and find that they're grasping at fog. Some are then driven to say that Zen isn't real, that it's some kind of con and people involved in it are deluding themselves. But fog is real. Just because you can't grab a handful doesn't mean that you doubt its existence. It's just that you have to accept that it's different from, say, a chunk of wood, and has to be dealt with differently.

For the writer it is very hard indeed not to say misleading things. Everything you say is provisional and imperfect. At the very least you are constantly aware of complications that haven't been explained. But if you try to explain them all, the whole subject will become so utterly complicated that you'd end up explaining nothing.

That is why Zen masters were notably terse in their comments. They tended to hint and suggest rather than explain. Zen is full of aphorisms, anecdotes, and poems. It is rather short on learned essays (there are some but they are mainly impenetrable). This is a good approach but it depends on readers who are already, to some extent, on the same wavelength. What is interesting to me is that Zen could be of help to people who don't think of themselves as Oriental culture buffs, who may not even think they are particularly "religious" (whatever that means). To reach people like that I have taken some risks. I've put things in a way I hope they'll find interesting and accessible.

To add to the dilemma, I'm British, and the bulk of my readers are going to be American. This demands some serious thought on my part. Zen is a very personal business and to talk about how it relates to you, I need to tell you how it relates to me. It isn't a coldly factual subject like electronics or double-entry bookkeeping. If I pretend to be an American you'll see through me in a moment and lose interest. On the other hand, a book that's all about Britain will just seem foreign and inapplicable. I've tried to bridge the Atlantic as best I can. Let's hope none of us end up in the ocean.

So, this is it—a series of Zen snapshots. I intended them to be interesting and useful, and I hope that to some extent I've succeeded. On all other important points I reserve the right to change my mind.

# Unlearning Zen

## Dumping the excess baggage

Usually, when you investigate some new interest, you start by accumulating knowledge. You carry out research on the Internet, read books and magazines, search the schedules for TV shows, talk to people who are already involved, or maybe join an evening class or sign up for a college class. When you start to take an interest in Zen you do the same thing. It's only natural, the way you've been taught since childhood, and that is why you go marching off in quite the wrong direction. Because Zen is different. Of course, you can find out *about* Zen by all the usual methods but, if you want to get to the essence of Zen itself, you have to abandon that kind of search.

At this point you find yourself faced with a dilemma. No one, not even those born in countries where Zen is native, knows about it without study. If you talk to young Japanese people you will often find that they know next to nothing and find your interest mildly eccentric. So you

have no choice but to learn about the history of Buddhism, the development of the various schools, the way in which Zen evolved, the sayings of the great masters, the koans and the teaching stories. All this is necessary in a way, but it is also distracting you from what you really need, which is the direct experience of Zen. There is nothing that is more practical, less theoretical, and completely based on your personal experience than Zen is. It is also decidedly quirky.

If you've ever taught a child to read, you'll know that it is not a straightforward procedure. There is a multitude of "approved" methods that come into fashion and then frequently go out again just as quickly. But whether you favor phonics, "Look and Say," "real books," or whatever, you will soon realize that in one sense none of these methods really works.

Each is, at best, an approximate description of how to read. The actual process remains mysterious. The child will dutifully intone "C—A—T is CAT," but, of course, it isn't that simple. Sooner or later, the child makes an intuitive leap and manages to turn the sounds into words. In any language this process is a great and wonderful mystery, but in English, with its mass of inconsistencies and irregularities, it approaches the miraculous. But it happens, and it happens frequently and regularly.

Zen is not dissimilar. Everything that you are told about Zen is approximately true, and is given to you by people who have only the most earnest desire to be of help. Sadly, they are not able to convey to you the precise experience they are talking about. There is another peculiarity that needs explaining. If we return to our reading analogy, once you have the knack of it, your reading gets better as you learn more and more. In Zen, the opposite applies: You throw knowledge out. My favorite analogy for this is that it's like unlearning a language. If you've ever learnt a language you'll know how you acquire the knowledge bit by bit, day by day, until your hesitant gabbling finally turns into something people can understand. Now think of the process in reverse. Zen involves throwing out concepts, discarding preconceptions, dispensing with prejudices, clearing your mental closets of all the junk you've collected during the course of your life. It's a long process but, at some point—as with reading—something clicks. It is only by experience that you will be able to turn Z—E—N into Zen.

# Zen doesn't bite

Just dive in, there are no sharks

Zen has a reputation for being difficult. This is partly because Zen masters are constitutionally incapable of giving straight answers to what enquirers think are perfectly reasonable questions. A seemingly simple question like "What is Zen?" will usually elicit an incomprehensible response. Then there are all those koans, the questions that Zen masters set for their pupils to help them along the road to enlightenment. Only they are not regular questions. "What was your original face before you were born?" "What is the sound of one hand clapping?" "There is a goose in a bottle. How do you get it out without breaking the bottle?" It soon becomes apparent that normal logical processes are not going to be much use with questions like these. Some people get quite angry about it. An acquaintance of mine spent ages on the telephone pointing out to me that language and reason are two of the foundation stones of society and any attempt to undermine them would have drastic consequences for civilization. I had a hard time convincing her that Zen was not a subversive movement.

Some people would be prepared to give Zen a try but then they see the way in which almost nothing the pupil says will ever satisfy the teacher. This can be just plain dispiriting. We are used to the link between effort and praise, between struggle and achievement. The idea of trying very hard and then being told that you are barking up the wrong tree does not sit well with most Westerners.

Getting it wrong is a really important part of Zen. In life, you learn nothing without making mistakes, but in Zen your learning will be one long mistake. This is really OK. The problem is that Zen does not work like any of the other things we learn. It does not follow the equation

*more knowledge = more understanding.*

Eventually you get used to the idea that you will never really understand Zen.

At least not in the way that you might understand how to fix your computer, or speak Russian, or explain quantum theory. These are subjects that, however difficult they might be, can all be understood by using the same basic method. You could go to the library, get out a book, and study any of them until you reach the level of understanding you require. But Zen isn't like that. You could read every book in the library and feel as if you were no further forward.

*Zen is like riding a bike. You don't learn to do it by acquiring knowledge; you learn to do it by doing it.*

Zen is more like riding a bike. You don't learn to do it by acquiring knowledge; you learn to do it by doing it. "Hang on tight and pedal like hell!" my dad yelled as he launched me on my first attempt at cycling. It wasn't a great body of knowledge but it told me all the essentials I needed. When you've learnt to ride a bike, you just do it. You don't understand how you do it. In fact, if someone asked you to explain the process logically, you'd be unable to explain. And the falling-off is an important part of learning. Getting that sense of balance is a lot to do with what you *don't* do.

So Zen is a lot like that. It doesn't matter one bit if you get it wrong. However, it would matter quite a lot if you never gave it a try.

# He ain't heavy, he's my Buddha

## What was Buddha like?
## Is he still relevant today?

I discovered Buddha when I was about fifteen, and we clicked immediately. There are some people you just know you're going to get along with. When it comes to religious leaders I'm pretty hard to please. I'd had a standard Scots Protestant upbringing, but somehow had never really felt at home with Jesus. I'd liked the Bible stories well enough. If you lived in Edinburgh, a cold, grey, windy city for much of the year, you'd understand the appeal of stories about Roman Palestine, all sun, sand, and palm trees.

The thing I liked about Buddha was his total confidence. He didn't say, "I'm the Son of God and you'd better listen to what I have to say," or "I got this straight from the Archangel Gabriel and if you don't take notice you're in big trouble." All he said was that he was an ordinary man who had, through strenuous efforts, become enlightened. He'd actually

21

found the answer to human suffering and how to end it. Then he said that anyone could do the same if they followed the path he described. But that wasn't the best part. What really impressed me was when he said that I shouldn't trust any teachers (not even him,) but that I should go and find out for myself. As far as I was concerned, that clinched the deal then and there. Over the years I have put his "try it for yourself" clause to every test imaginable. I've never felt the need to adopt beliefs just because they were thought to be what Buddhists are (according to some people) supposed to follow. I've been, frankly, sceptical about almost everything. Much of the stuff that many of my fellow Buddhists embrace with enthusiasm, I've thrown out as useless or irrelevant. It's not that I'm naturally cussed or contrary, but I take the ideas of "try it for yourself" and "don't trust teachers" extremely seriously. I think of these as jewels of Buddhism, and feel sorry for religions that need to surround themselves with fences to make sure that no one strays.

Once I was in Jerusalem and was describing to a colleague, a Roman Catholic monk, the Tibetan Buddhist wedding ceremony that had followed our first, more conventional, wedding. He was a broad-minded man and had no difficulty with the idea that I was not a member of his faith. Then a thought struck him and he asked how the Tibetan lama had known that I was a genuine Buddhist. The answer, "Because I told him so," visibly shocked him. When it transpired that Buddhism did not have any real equivalent to baptism or confirmation he got quite upset. It hadn't really occurred to me before that this was a major difference between Buddhists and others. If you're a Buddhist then you are on a journey of exploration with other people, but you don't have to wear the same clothes, eat the same food, or even think the same thoughts. You can even take the odd detour and rejoin the others further down the line. I suppose at some point you might become so separated from the crowd that you wouldn't be recognizable as a Buddhist anymore,

but I've never seen it happen.

There's no such thing as a lapsed Buddhist.

23

# Zen and cartography

## The importance of your mental maps

Most people turn to religion to find some degree of certainty in their lives. They want to find answers to the important questions, such as "Why am I here?," "What should I do with my life?," "What is life all about?" Many religions put great emphasis on faith. You believe things and do things because you have faith in your God, in your holy book, in your prophets, and in your religious teachers. Zen isn't like this. In Zen there is talk of Great Faith, but it is different. It is really just a rock-solid belief that, if you follow it steadfastly enough, Zen will lead to enlightenment. There is no sense in which this faith extends to particular dogmas or practices. In Zen, Great Faith goes hand in hand with Great Doubt, which means just what it says—you have to cultivate doubt to the point when you don't even know where to put your foot next. This often seems strange to outsiders.

Psychologists encourage us to be flexible in the making of what they call our "mental maps." Your map is your version of reality; it is what you believe about yourself, your life, your work, your relationships. According to many psychologists it is a sign of robust mental health if you are willing to alter or even completely redraw your map in the light of experience. Some people find this difficult. They get to a stage in life when they feel that they have worked out their relationships, their political and religious opinions, their place in society, and they want to stop right there. They feel threatened and get angry if anyone suggests that any further changes are called for.

Zen is only for people who are willing to redraw their map constantly. It is hard to say anything about Zen that you don't regret later. Nothing that you can *say* will ever

be true in more than a very provisional way. You soon get to realize that much of Zen is to do with making mistakes. You throw away one misconception after another. You try as hard as you can to get closer to the truth but you must never make the mistake of getting to a position that seems final and then try to rest there.

> Your map is your version of reality; it is what you believe about yourself, your life, your work, your relationships.

As you continue on your journey, you develop a deeper understanding. Or rather, you throw away many ineffective and unworkable beliefs, and the more mental garbage you throw out, the closer you get to the truth. Zen is far more about what isn't than what is.

I once worked for a cartographic publisher. Until I got the job, I hadn't really given maps much thought. It hadn't occurred to me that cartography was a never-ending process. Every now and then we would publish an atlas but it was always, in a sense, provisional and out of date, even before it hit the bookshops. In the backrooms of our offices there would be a team of cartographers beavering away, constantly updating the information and producing newer and better versions of the maps. In this way cartography has much in common with Zen. When you have reached an understanding that you're satisfied with, throw it away! And you will be one step closer to the truth.

# Chocolate in the here and now

## How to live in the present

I once visited a man in prison. Visitors weren't allowed to take anything in for the prisoners, but over to one side of the interview room was a little serving hatch where you could buy refreshments. I bought us two coffees and two chocolate bars (both for him as I was trying to lose weight —again). What impressed me was the way he ate the chocolate. Our conversation stopped dead as he nibbled it very slowly and carefully, relishing every little morsel.
I realized the difference it makes when something becomes special to you. I could buy chocolate every day and wolf it down without thinking. For him it was a special occasion, like a birthday.

Zen places great emphasis on living in the here and now. Some people make the mistake of thinking this is the same as "living for the moment," trying to get as much fun as you can out of life because it might not last. But that's not it. The point of living in the here

29

By insisting on
mindfulness, Zen tries
to help us end our
confusion and live
simply and effectively.

and now is that life is special and miraculous but, because we get bogged down in routine and spend time sorting out endless problems, we often lose sight of how great it is. There is an old piece of advice: "Live as if you'll live forever, but live each day as though it were your last." Yet this is only part of what we mean by here and now.

The next part is more complicated. Right at *this* moment you have no problems. I can hear some of you screaming at me, "I just lost my job!," "I just found that I have heart trouble!" But, I repeat, at this moment you have no problems. Problems come when you begin to mull things over in your mind, construct complicated ideas about your life, and worry about what's going to happen next. Let's say that you're ill and in pain. Most of your problem comes not from the pain but from your confusion over what will happen to you, and what that will mean for your family and friends. Pain is just pain: you don't have to like it, but it's quite simple. When you've got it you're not in any confusion over what you feel. The trouble is that humans are not very good at living in the moment. Animals seem to do it with no effort. As far as we can tell, they don't care much for introspection. But we humans do little else. And the more we think about "what if?" and "what then?," the more confused and miserable we get. By insisting on mindfulness, Zen tries to help us end our confusion and live simply and effectively.

# I'm really stuck on you

## Talking about non-attachment

Zen makes a big issue of attachment. You can become attached to almost anything; love, sex, anger, greed, and possessions are just a handful of examples. The most obvious attachments are the "bad" ones. It is easy to see when people are attached to anger, for example, when they get stuck in a fight in which neither side will back off. Lives have been ruined, and even ended, by attachments of that sort. You also see people clinging desperately to money and possessions, oblivious to the old saying about there being no pockets in a shroud. However strongly people feel such attachments and are misled by them, it is comparatively easy for others to see the mistake and avoid them. But other attachments are harder to avoid.

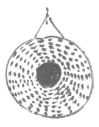

There is, for example, the attachment to oneself. Your own life can easily seem so important and significant that you can get stuck on it. I know a fellow writer, like me someone who makes a living from his efforts but is

unlikely to go down in history, yet he chronicles his life as though preparing it for some future biographer. He logs all his telephone calls, keeps immaculate diaries of his deeds, compiles a huge bibliography of his work, and chats quite happily about his significance (and, at least by implication, it is a *great* significance) to the world of books. No one has the heart to tell him.

It's easy to look askance at attachments of this sort. But what about the "good" attachments? What about love, for example? I don't mean the Romeo and Juliet, erotic, obsessive sort of love, I mean the nice, religiously respectable, husband-wife-and-two-kids sort. Surely that is not only blameless but meritorious? It's the sort of thing that politicians commend when they decide to get on the "family values" bandwagon.

The trouble is that even that form of attachment ends in suffering. Couples, however devoted, are separated by death. There is a Zen saying that evil-doers suffer as evil-doers, but good people suffer as good people. This is one of the reasons that Buddhism was so strongly rooted in the monastic tradition. If you don't make attachments

# What Buddhists strive for is not detachment but non-attachment.

to other people, the theory ran, you won't entangle yourself in suffering. This led to Buddhism being regarded as a religion that cultivates detachment, a rather cold aloofness from the everyday world. But that isn't true.

What Buddhists strive for is not detachment but non-attachment. This is much more difficult. It involves being able to live without getting "stuck" to things and people along the way. Every day you have to realize that life is fleeting and that there is nowhere solid for you to settle down and rest. To many people this sounds terrible, and it certainly isn't easy but it is, I think, the only conclusion that any sensible person can reach. It doesn't mean that you drift through life not caring about others— quite the reverse. Our shared fragility is one of the things that makes everyone so special and important. I don't for a moment claim to have mastered non-attachment. I don't know if I ever will. But I know that I have to keep trying.

# Pain is so close to pleasure

Are our pleasures just another sort of pain?

We spend a lot of time and effort trying to fill our lives with pleasure. The things that give us pleasure are many and varied: food, beauty, sex, warmth, light, excitement, comfort, escapism—the list could be a very long one. Our aim is always to gravitate toward pleasure and keep away from pain. Life contains quite a lot of pain, including everything from mild annoyance and discomfort to major illness, injury, and death. At the back of our minds we know that, in the end, pain wins. Do what you like, you're going to end up, if you're lucky, old, sick, and then dead. If you're unlucky, the pain can finish you off much sooner. These are uncomfortable thoughts and, to avoid them for as long as possible, pleasure is the antidote of choice.

To some extent it works. If you tickle your pleasure zones often enough, life can seem pretty sweet. The trouble is that a lot of the things that give us pleasure can also lead to pain. Escaping the pain of everyday life through alcohol and drugs, for example, can easily become

37

a route to more pain. The same goes for many of the other ways we try to distract ourselves. Too often, what we call "pleasure" is simply a refined form of pain. Look at fairgrounds and theme park white knuckle rides and you'll see what I mean. That may be an extreme example, but there are plenty of other ways in which we use what is really a mild form of pain as a source of pleasure.

What has this got to do with Zen? It is important because Zen teaches us to look life full in the face. Some people think that the Buddhist insistence on old age, suffering, and death is morbid and depressing. Buddhists simply think of it as realistic.

Once you see that pleasures are
ephemeral (as are many pains,)
you start to appreciate life.

Zen training helps us to see beyond dualities such as pain and pleasure; it shows that clinging to one and shunning the other is simply playing the same old worn-out game over and over. Once you see that pleasures are ephemeral (as are many pains,) you start to appreciate life in a way that no longer involves playing the pain/pleasure game. Your whole life is a miracle. Even a lot of the things that most people want to avoid (like waiting for the bus on a cold, wet morning) are miraculous. Zen helps you to appreciate the whole of your life and to discard purely artificial distinctions such as pain and pleasure.

# Zen and positive thinking

Is thinking positive such a good idea?

In recent times an outbreak of positive thinking has swept the world. What started out as a bit of fashionable psychobabble has taken root in our consciousness and flourished remarkably. Now you not only hear sports personalities, film stars, pop stars, and all sorts of public figures reminding us solemnly of the need to "stay positive," but ordinary people going about their everyday lives also intone this mantra. I even heard a couple of school kids on a bus, talking about a mid-term test. One of them doubted whether she'd get a good grade but her friend had the answer: "You've just got to remember to stay positive."

The idea of people being constantly hopeful, optimistic, enthusiastic, and cheerful in adversity is an attractive one. It certainly beats the hell out of gloom and doom. But the thinking that underlies this idea needs closer examination. The taste for positivity goes back much further than the current fashion. In the

West we think of things in contrasting pairs and, both consciously and unconsciously, we choose the positive and reject the negative. So we prefer life to death, love to hate, peace to war, beauty to ugliness, and truth to falsehood. That's how it should be, isn't it? No, not really.

The Chinese also used to classify things into contrasting pairs, which they called Yin and Yang. They represented this in a diagram. You've almost certainly seen it because all sorts of people have now adopted the Yin–Yang as some kind of good luck symbol, but do they know what it really means? The two sides of the diagram remind us of fish, each holding the tail of the other in its mouth. The white side has a black dot and the black side a white dot. Why? Because each side has the seed of the other in it. If everything was white, how would we know about black? White only exists in contrast to black. All the pairs depend on each other for their existence. For the Chinese, the Western dualistic attitude is nonsense.

After the September 11 terrorist attacks, broadcast media immediately banned items that might be considered to be in bad taste. Among the casualties was Louis Armstrong's "What a Wonderful World." How could you allow someone to sing a lyric like that when thousands of people lay dead? Of course, the lyric had always been ridiculous. At any time when the song was sung there must have been millions of people dying of starvation, or homeless, or persecuted, or living in desperate poverty. Clearly positive thinking is OK as long as you don't take it too far.

Zen teaches us to take life, and death, as they come. Making divisions, preferring one thing to another, trying to grab at some things while avoiding others, is not the way to understanding. The habit, which we have had drummed into us from childhood, is hard to break. You want to be warm, not cold, you want to be fed, not hungry, you want to be happy, not sad. If you make the effort you find that your attitudes will change. You begin to see that the differences you used to be so keen on are not real, they are merely concepts. Beyond them is the real world and you can reach it by not constantly making choices.

43

# Tea time with Hitler

## Zen and evil people

Well, would you? Have tea with Hitler, I mean. Or Charles Manson maybe, or the Marquis de Sade? No, of course not. We tend to think of ourselves as "ordinary, decent people" and to recoil from evil, from those who have put themselves beyond the pale. In fact there is a whole social convention that insists that such people are radically different from the rest of us. People say things like "they behaved like animals" (even though animals would be most unlikely to do some of the nastier things humans get up to.) There is also an idea, heavily promoted by the tabloid press, that such people are "monsters." This is a really useful concept because it saves us considering uncomfortable issues too closely. Nothing to do with us— let Buffy the Vampire Slayer go deal with it.

Zen takes a radically different view, which is that the original nature of our mind is pure. How can that be? Surely people who have committed heinous crimes cannot possibly have a pure mind?

What's the matter with these Zen types, are they just a
bunch of wimpy liberals? No, they're not. On matters of
morality Zen is pretty uncompromising. The standards that
Zen people expect of themselves are rigorous ones. The
difference is that, from a Zen point of view, the evil is not
something that people *are*, it's something they acquire.
Something extra that gets added on but is not part of the
person. My favorite analogy is of someone who has been
rolling around in the mud. They're dirty all right, no doubt
about that. They may even be so utterly filthy that you
cannot recognize them as
human. But underneath
they are unchanged.

46

The dirt washes off. It might not be easy, and it could take an awful lot of hot, soapy water, but eventually they can come clean.

Is this true? The trouble is that, since most of us will never meet anyone on the far edge of evil, it's hard to say. What we can see in our own lives is that people who do bad things are usually sad and stupid rather than evil. I've met many, many silly, thoughtless, opportunist, selfish people, but none that I would really class as evil. The trouble is that it is quite easy to start behaving badly, thinking that no one will find out, and then to become sucked into behaving badly on a routine basis. I watched a former colleague of mine, a nice kindly man, who was, however, never quite able to master the distinction between "mine" and "yours," slide gently down the slope until he lost his job and, eventually, killed himself.

Surely there is a difference between people who do ordinary bad things (lying, cheating, stealing) and those who, for example, commit murder? I've only ever met one murderer. In prison he discovered a talent for proofreading and, for some time, my company gave him work. His story was not a catalogue of evil, just a sorry tale of inability to cope. He'd become highly stressed, turned to drink and drugs, got into an argument with a stranger, and killed him. Evil? Hardly. He was one of the saddest, most pathetic people I ever met. His considerable talents would never be put to any serious use because of an incident of pure stupidity.

# The karma of cholesterol

Reflections on the law of causation

I visited the doctor to get the result of my cholesterol test. The reading was so high she thought for a moment she was looking at my telephone number. Was this a punishment for excessive cheese consumption? A well-merited slap on the wrist for greed? No, it wasn't. But it was karma.

People raised in the Judaeo-Christian culture often find karma a difficult concept. They have been brought up to expect reward for good behavior and punishment for sins. Even people with no very strong belief in God often feel that the world works in this way. The first thing that strikes them as odd about karma is that there is no averaging out of good and bad behaviour. According to this Eastern concept, good acts bring good results and bad acts bring suffering, and all your good and bad acts count. Keeping up a good average doesn't excuse you from the result of your blunders.

The next thing Westerners find odd is the fact that whereas they see God being in direct charge of the rewards and punishments, in the East karma is regarded as a natural law, like gravity. If you drop a hammer on your toe it hurts. This is not a "punishment" for carelessness, but it may teach you to be more careful with that hammer in future. My cholesterol check has taught me to go easy on the cheese in future. Is this a lesson in health or morality? Is there a difference?

Unfortunately the original idea of karma has over time become confused in many people's minds with the Judaeo-Christian system. Many less educated people in the East now believe that a sinful life will result in bad karma and a bad rebirth. This unsubtle and untrue belief has spread back to the West. This is really not what karma is all about.

People who are careless about the way they live their lives build up a whole heap of suffering for themselves. As you get older you can see this happen.

One of my elderly relatives now lives out a pointless and unhappy old age, acutely aware of the fact that he never put his life to any real use, spent his time on things that were amusing but essentially futile, and now feels that, as he puts it, he "wasted his go."

> People who are careless about the way they live their lives build up a whole heap of suffering for themselves.

Viewed correctly, karma is a learning process rather than a punitive one. We get what we need in order to grow. As long as we regard ourselves as being punished, we are missing the point. If we push forward skillfully, then our lives make progress toward enlightenment. However, we have to be able to look out for warning signs that tell us when we are on the wrong track.

There is a Zen story of a monk condemned to spend many reincarnations as a fox because he had got hold of the idea that an enlightened man is above karma. It took a Zen master to point out to him that the enlightened man is actually *in tune* with karma.

A clear conscience is certainly a wonderful thing, but skillful karma is better. If you feel that you have the wind in your sails and that your life is going in the right direction, as if in spite of the years you are still young at heart, as if the force of life is somehow on your side, then it is likely that your karma is in good shape. Enjoy the journey!

# Up to the elbows in Zen suds

## The pleasures of everyday chores

Just as we were about to get married, my bride-to-be
mentioned that she liked to listen to pop music on the
radio while washing up or ironing. I was young, foolish,
and full of enthusiasm (which my beloved did not share)
for Zen. In a reckless moment I suggested that, if she left
off the pop music, she might actually enjoy what she was
doing instead of letting her mind wander aimlessly. Yes, it
was a stupid thing to say. It naturally led to a row, tears,
and recriminations. Served me right. Like many Zen
adherents I was fully aware of the need to
cultivate Mindfulness without being too clear
what it actually was. All Buddhists talk a lot
about the need to live in the Here and Now,
and they devote considerable effort to trying
to do just that.

It isn't easy. The big mistake people make is to
confuse mindfulness with concentration. They
struggle gamely to focus their entire mental

Mindfulness comes when you
are so fully involved in what
you are doing that you and
the activity become one.

energy on completing some simple task. They feel guilty
about letting their mind wander. Some teachers actually
encourage this attitude and set their students exercises
aimed at increasing their concentration. This is all a huge
waste of time and effort.

   Mindfulness comes when you are so fully involved in
what you are doing that you and the activity become one.
This is a completely different feeling because it involves no
strain on your part, no warding off of the "wrong"
thoughts. If you drive a car you'll know what I mean.
People talk about how important it is to concentrate, but
when you drive you actually don't concentrate on what
you are doing at all. If you really had to think about each
of your actions, you wouldn't be able to drive. That's why
learners find it so hard, because they really *do* think,
"Change gear, press the accelerator, signal right, slow
down." And we all know that isn't proper driving. A good
driver feels at one with the vehicle, and is so used to
making the car do what's needed that there is no need to
think in that awkward, one-thing-at-a-time fashion at all.

Why does all this matter? Whether you're driving or washing the dishes, surely all that matters is the end result. But that's not so. The trouble with the way most people think is that it helps to preserve the illusion that the universe is made up of separate bits all banging around in something called "space." If you cultivate one-at-a-time thinking it is impossible to become aware of the wholeness of things. You might, in a theoretical kind of way, believe that everything is part of the whole, but you'll never feel it in your bones. If you become mindful then you will see just how marvelously all the bits are part of the One. And you might even learn to enjoy washing up.

# Everyone's a Buddha, baby!

Can it *really* be true?

One of the things people like about Buddhism is that everyone is, by definition, a fully qualified Buddha or, and this is the important difference, a *potential* Buddha. Zen insists that you can't really go out and get enlightened because you're already enlightened, you just don't realize it yet. This is a comforting thought.

Now go and stand on a corner in your local shopping mall and watch the people pass you by. Do you *really* believe they are all potential Buddhas? What, even the guy with the "Satan's Slave" tattoo and the interesting body piercings, and the woman who's busy giving one of her kids a wallop with one hand while trying to light another cigarette with the other? Even the people who think of nothing more than fast food, trash TV, booze, and easy sex? Even the petty thieves and dropouts?

Maybe I'm just being too ready to judge people by appearances. I mean, it's possible that Satan's Slave spends his time helping disabled kids, or running a shelter for the homeless. OK, I admit that appearances can sometimes be deceptive, but not always, not even most of the time. Most of the time people are pretty much what they appear to be.

The trouble is that it's quite easy to see nice people as Buddhas in waiting. The sort of people who think about moral issues, who want to live a good life, who care about their relationships, look after their families, and fret about how to attain World Peace—all these seem like Buddha material. But the vast bulk of humanity isn't nice. They aren't even really nasty, they're just a heap of disorganized appetites that are struggling to be satisfied. It's not hard to see why some of our writers and philosophers have found humanity a pretty dismal prospect.

This is the really good bit of Zen. Once you start to look for good in people, you find it.

There is no easy answer to this one. There really is no nice pat little bit of fortune-cookie philosophy that suddenly makes it OK. Zen does, however, eventually come to the rescue. The odd thing about Zen is that it has a way of changing things for you from the inside. Outwardly, everything remains just the same. No angels descend from heaven singing "Hallelujah." But people and things start to glow a little from the inside. You do begin to detect that things are not quite as discouraging as you once thought. More importantly, your own attitudes begin to change.

This is the really good bit of Zen. Once you start to look for good in people, you find it. Once you really begin to expect Buddhas, you get Buddhas. And people will pick up your attitude and pass it on. Try this experiment. Next time you're in a line of traffic and other people are trying to join the line, stop and let someone in. Then watch that person to see what happens. Nine times out of ten they'll take the next possible opportunity to pass on the good deed. OK, it's a tiny example and it won't change the world, but repeat it enough times in different ways and you'll make a difference. Then maybe you'll start to see Buddhas where you used to see bums.

# Zen and the art of mountaineering

## A surprise for the self-directed

Zen tends to appeal to tough-minded, independent types, the sort of people who like to be in charge of their own lives. Maybe that's why when it came West it settled so happily in the U.S., a land where sturdy independence and the pioneer spirit live on. Psychologists call this attitude "internal locus of control," and recognize it as a very valuable personality trait. If you look at the history of Zen you find it littered with formidable characters who were undaunted even in the most difficult situations. Zen masters were more than a match for anyone they encountered, no matter how exalted they might be—even samurai, who held an absolute right to kill those who obstructed them, would think twice before picking a fight with a Zen monk and, when they did, they ended up regretting it. There are even tales of the odd Emperor getting the rough edge of a Zen master's tongue.

I sometimes think that Zen is a bit like climbing a mountain. It can certainly feel that way. It's not just the struggle up the sheer rock face of reality, though that's daunting enough. There is also that feeling you get in the mountains when, as soon as you have conquered one summit, you see another rising above you, issuing a new challenge. Zen also gives you a feeling of danger, of grappling with something bigger and stronger than you are and which, if things go wrong, could end up hurting you.

Of course, because this is Zen, nothing is ever straightforward—you know that there will be a sting in the tail somewhere. The sting is this: there is no mountain. The thing you are struggling up so laboriously does not exist. Not only that but, no matter how hard you try, you will never get to grips with Zen by making that sort of effort.

So, what do you do? Give up? No—if you give up you'll never get there. Making the effort is important. When I'm not writing for a living, I sometimes teach creative writing to others. The most important thing to get across to students of writing is that waiting for inspiration is useless. First you have to put in the effort, even if you feel that that effort is not producing the results you wanted. When you have tried and tried and tried then, even if your results have been disappointing, you will often find that after all the rubbish has been cleared from your mind you'll be rewarded with some nuggets of genuine creativity that spring from the deep inner recesses of your consciousness.

Zen works like that too. The object of koan study is to force the student to make strenuous and useless efforts to

understand that which cannot be grasped by normal means. The fact that the effort is useless does not mean that *making* it is not important. If you don't go through that experience you will never find the answer.

Let's go back to those formidable Zen masters. It is important to understand that they did not behave as they did out of arrogance and belief in their own power. They were not spiritual versions of some Wild West hero. Their strength came from having thrown away the mental props that most of us lean on. But the act of accepting their lack of personal power liberated them and made them invincible in a different way. They climbed mountains.

# Just who do you think you are?

## The importance of knowing yourself

"Just be yourself!" is advice we often give to those nervous about appearing in public for the first time. It's one of those stupid, self-contradictory pieces of advice, like "Just relax!" or "Don't worry!" Being yourself is not something you can do by trying, nor is it all that easy. For many people, knowing who they are is a major problem. I'm sure you can think of people who are firmly convinced that they are kindly, or intelligent, or creative, or great lovers, or possess many other wonderful attributes but, in fact, are completely mistaken. This is a great mystery. Many people have a genius for ignoring their own faults while awarding themselves Brownie points for great talents and virtues they do not really possess. Even more mysterious, I know people who do not even know what they like and dislike. My elderly aunt would regularly plan holidays that she was convinced she desperately needed only to return home disappointed. What she forgot each year was simply that she *hated* holidays.

It gets stranger. One of the most selfish, self-deluding, and misguided people I know spends most of his spare time reading books bought from the Mind, Body, Spirit shelf and chasing enlightenment with huge, but ineffectual, energy. His conversation majors on his own advanced spiritual condition, which he loves to contrast with the appalling inadequacy of others.

This raises a serious problem. How do any of us know that we are not doing just the same? How can we be sure that it is not us who are out of touch and deluded? It's a tough one but, if you want to make any kind of spiritual progress, it's a question that has to be faced. You can seek professional help from a psychiatrist or therapist but, as a therapist friend once told me, "I can't *make* people accept truths about themselves that they aren't ready to accept."

I think one important clue is to look at the people around you and see what they think of you. Do people gravitate toward you or shy away? Do they ask your advice or ignore it? Do they trust you or not? Of course, even this test has to be applied with care. It could easily be allowed

to become a popularity contest, and we all know that it's easy to be popular without having any real moral qualifications. So you need to choose your people with care and, sure enough, if you're the self-deluding kind, you'll soon scare up a posse of sycophants who'll support your view.

The situation is difficult but not impossible. Many people *do* know themselves and they understand their strengths and struggle to eliminate their weaknesses. But for Zen this is only the first phase; it is a mere prerequisite for finding out who you *really* are.

Of all the koans Zen students use during zazen, the one that appears the simplest must be "Who am I?" The answer is not the one you reach through the sort of soul-searching we've discussed so far in this chapter. You need to go through that stage because, unless you have, you'll never get near the real answer. In Zen, knowing who you are involves delving into your personality and discovering that it is a trick. That there is no "real you" but only an illusion. It's like peeling an onion. You strip away layer after layer, pretense after pretense. And what do you find when you have stripped away all the layers of the onion? No onion.

# Of mice and Zen

## Can we afford to be harmless?

We live in a fen village. It isn't one of those pretty English villages with thatched cottages with roses round the door, but a real farming community. It smells of pigs, chickens, or sheep, depending on the direction of the wind. Our cottage is right on the edge of farmland and we get mice, lots of them. At a personal level, I rather like mice but in the fall, as the weather gets colder, they decide to invade the house. There is no way you can live with mice in your house. One or two may seem cute but two soon become a multitude. Also, they start to invade the kitchen. I don't begrudge them the food but they make everything dirty. Anything they've touched has to be thrown out.

So what to do? Humane traps, you might think, are the answer. But they aren't. First, mice are pretty streetwise and can see a humane trap for what it is (trust me, I've tried the experiment with both types of trap and they fling themselves recklessly on the old-fashioned ones while avoiding the others.) Also, assuming you catch your mouse humanely, what do you do with it?

Even if I eat exclusively vegetarian food, do you really think that the farmers who produced it didn't kill pests and vermin to protect their crops?

Throw it back into the yard? It would find its way in again within hours, if not minutes. Dump it in a field? That might make me feel better but it doesn't do much for the mouse. According to a zoologist friend, a mouse out of its own territory is, sooner rather than later, a dead mouse.

So I use traps and I kill mice. My neighbors would laugh themselves silly at the thought that this causes me pangs of conscience. Farmers have a short way with vermin. But Buddhists are supposed to save all sentient beings, including mice. So am I just a bad Buddhist?

The whole issue of harmlessness is much more complex than people think. It is easy to go through the motions. You can refuse to fight, refuse to kill, refuse to eat meat. Lots of Buddhists are pacifist vegetarians. But does that really get you off the hook? I think the truth is that merely by living I condemn other creatures, and people, to die. The world as it is organized does not have enough resources to go around. By living in the affluent West I am inflicting poverty, famine, and death on people I've never met who live in the Third World. Also, even if I eat exclusively vegetarian food, do you really think that the farmers who produced it didn't kill pests and vermin to protect their crops? I am glad that Buddhism places such great emphasis on doing no harm. I think that in most circumstances it is the right way to act. But, I'm sorry; when you get down to the nitty-gritty, no one is harmless.

# Navel-gazing for beginners

## What is Zazen?

Meditation, which is so deeply rooted in eastern countries that it has, over the millennia, developed a whole multitude of types, styles, and purposes, is so little known in the West that it has only one all-purpose and frequently misunderstood name. To make matters worse, somewhere along the line somebody got hold of the idea that these mystical Orientals sit around all day contemplating their own navels. What idiots! What utter nonsense! So "navel-gazing" has become the accepted shorthand for a sort of excessive and useless self-absorption. This is a great pity, since a little navel-gazing might just help some of our self-styled rationalists to be a little less bumptious.

Meditation was seen and remarked upon by visitors to the East right from the beginning. Naturally, what people noticed most were the more extreme manifestations.

Accounts of early explorers are full of stories about monks who could sit motionless and apparently oblivious while needles were stuck into their flesh or incense sticks glued to their skin and set alight. No one appeared to give much thought to what purpose such practices might serve. It was sufficient that they were odd and, preferably, inexplicable by scientific means. Although there was some early interest in Buddhism and, in the  nineteenth century, Madame Blavatsky and her Theosophists did make genuine (though somewhat erratic) efforts to understand Eastern thought, for the most part it was all considered rather odd and reprehensible. The Western response was that they were all ripe for conversion to Christianity, and the quicker the better.

Then in the 1960s the Beatles met the Maharishi Mahesh Yogi, who was popularizing a technique he called Transcendental Meditation. TM had huge advantages over other techniques, and put meditation firmly on the agenda as far as millions of Westerners were concerned. Not only was it promoted by the most influential rock band in history, but it was simple to learn, took up only a little of one's time, and promised its practitioners huge advantages.

TM, we were told, would not only aid your spiritual growth, but would improve your health, make you more effective in your work, and, if enough people practiced it, would promote lower levels of crime and start to bring about world peace. This is not the place to go into all the claims that TM's adherents made for it.

Naturally skeptics and traditionalists mocked. Lord Hailsham, a British politician of the day, thundered that it would do people much more good to read the letters of St Paul than follow the teachings of the man he styled the "giggling guru." The trouble was, TM worked. No, maybe it didn't achieve world peace. Nor did it give instant enlightenment. But huge numbers of people who tried it did discover benefits that were clearly not just the product of an overactive imagination. Meditation had arrived in the West, and it was here to stay.

I've lived with Zen meditation for 25 years and can honestly say that, in all that time, I've never gazed at my navel once. It's a shame that many people in the West feel that there is something foreign, mystical, or just plain creepy about meditation. Either that or they seek to explain it away. Once, after a seminar I'd held for people interested in learning more about Zen, a man gave a knowledgeable chuckle and said, "Oh, of course, it's just self-hypnosis, isn't it?" No, it isn't. It's an excellent method of self-development, a tool that helps spiritual growth, and, if you haven't yet learned how to do it, why not give it a try?

# The unimportance of Zazen

## Sitting doing nothing

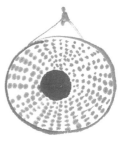

The one thing that everybody seems to know about Zen is that at its center is the practice of a form of meditation known as zazen. The sight of Japanese monks sitting motionless in orderly rows is somehow very impressive. When newcomers get interested in Zen they usually long to give zazen a try. Many of them go to great lengths to get it right. They feel that for it to be "the real thing" they have to master the lotus, or at least the half-lotus, position. For a Westerner this can be difficult and painful.

This is my first gripe. You're trying to learn about Zen, not taking a course in Japanese customs. These positions are fine for people who were born into a culture in which sitting cross-legged on the ground is a part of everyday life (and that, increasingly, does *not* include the Japanese, who are giving up the practice in droves.) For people who have never done such a thing before there seems little point in learning. Sitting cross-legged can obstruct blood flow and is not a good idea, especially if you're at the age where blood clots are a possibility. Instead, sit on an upright chair, but don't lean on it. Some people say that the traditional position gives "stability." Perhaps so, but when was the last time you fell off a chair?

Zazen itself is a wonderful experience. At first it's strange and difficult. We're really not used to spending time alone in this way. It's not even the same as introspection. In zazen you are not encouraged to think about anything except, perhaps, your koan. Some people experience problems with what they think of as "doing nothing." We in the West have a horror of being alone and inactive. That's why solitary confinement is always so feared by even the toughest criminals. But if you stick with it you find out that you are not "doing nothing" and that you are certainly not alone. Zazen does not cut you off from the rest of the world; it joins you to it. Your meditation stretches out and includes your surroundings.

Eventually you will get good at zazen and you'll look forward to every session. But that can, in itself, be a problem. Because Zen is not just zazen. You will hear people say that "everything you do is zazen," and, though at some level you might accept that this is so, you will probably feel, deep down, that zazen is "real" Buddhism where, say, mowing the lawn isn't. That is quite the wrong understanding. In fact everything you do really *is* zazen. Eventually zazen penetrates the marrow of your bones and

you could do without formal sitting if you really had to.
As long as you have some special Zen feeling or some part
of your life that is labeled Zen, you're missing the point.
When your Zen includes getting up in the morning, getting
washed, and urinating, then you understand.

Not long before he died, Alan W. Watts, a well-informed
and interesting writer on Eastern religion, wrote about how
he no longer meditated except when he really wanted to.
I was young at the time and shocked at what I considered
a terrible example of backsliding. But he was right. Zazen
is not a form of mental hygiene. It is not the spiritual
equivalent of cleaning your teeth. It needs to be done with
great care and purpose, and in the clear knowledge that it
is only one part of the Zen experience.

# Buddhist fundamentalism

To bow or not to bow?

My wife and I had two weddings, one Church of England, the other Tibetan Buddhist. Why not a Zen wedding? Because there is no Zen temple within easy reach of home, and the Tibetans, in that nice neighborly way that Buddhists have, were happy to offer us their hospitality. David, a non-Buddhist friend, came along to offer my non-Buddhist wife some moral support.

As we arrived, everyone was performing *puja* as a warm-up to the main event. We entered the prayer hall from the back and were faced with a sea of behinds as people made their bows to the Buddha. David, who fancies himself as a bit of a wit, murmured, "Is this an example of Buddhist fundamentalism?" For those who are not collectors of donnish humor, "fundament" is an archaic English word for buttocks.

In his way, my friend had highlighted one of the major misunderstandings that has

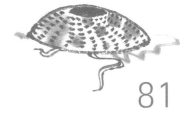

sullied relations between West and East for centuries. In the East it is important to show respect. Zen monks even bow to the cushion on which they meditate, because it is the place where, eventually, they hope to gain enlightenment and therefore is worthy of respect. This seems downright odd to Westerners, who often see prostrations as nothing more than spineless groveling.

Alexander the Great didn't help. When he took his army east, he noticed that monarchs in that neck of the woods were greeted by subjects prostrating themselves. He rather liked the idea and tried to get his rough and rugged Macedonians to do the same for him. Fat chance!

Matters were made no better when the British came to China to be informed that it was customary to *kow-tow* to the Emperor. Not one prostration but *nine*! The Emperor just *had* to be joking. He got a rather stiff bow from the shoulders and was expected to be grateful. We Brits know how to stop "Johnny Foreigner" getting above himself.

Zen is big on bowing. It goes hand in hand with zazen and chanting as one of the practices designed to promote spiritual growth. Some people, the ones who gulp down Japanese culture like strawberry ice-cream, take to it immediately. Others don't. Some take one look, are filled with genuine disgust, and stalk out never to return. They're not just being silly—it's just that in their culture, bowing is not a mark of respect, it's a sign of submission.

It's hard to explain to outsiders that, for Buddhists, the Buddha is not some sort of gilded idol you have to grovel to. He is *you*. At least he's the *real* you, the one that's hiding under all the layers of ignorance and pretense. The person you're bowing to is your true self. Unfortunately this explanation is undermined by some Buddhists who don't understand it themselves and who believe that the gilded statue is actually a representation of their god. I've had this argument with Thai friends (who have complicated and elaborate rules for the handling and treatment of Buddha images.) It usually turns into a "whose religion is it anyway?" sort of squabble.

I have to confess that, though I've done my share of *puja* in my time, I've never really felt entirely at home with the custom. I understand it intellectually but, somewhere in the background, there are Scottish ancestors yelling, "Get off yer knees ye great Jessie!" One's native culture dies hard.

83

# Should we become incensed?

## Smells and bells

An elderly English lady once wrote to a Buddhist journal complaining that the wrong sort of people were being attracted to Buddhism by the exotic trappings of incense, bells, and robes. Her suggested solution was that they should all be obliged to complete a two-year apprenticeship as Christians before being permitted to "graduate" to Buddhism. She was being silly, but she did have a point.

For some people the exotic nature of Buddhism is a powerful attraction. If you like spiritual fancy dress, then as a Buddhist you can really let it all hang out. These days incense is not quite as unusual as it once was. Every New Age fan seems to keep a stack of joss sticks handy, and you find that people light them at the slightest opportunity. But, of course, it all goes much, much further than that. You come across people who have been out and bought the entire kit: robes, bells, drums, you name it. They go even further and take on new names or teaching titles such as "Roshi." Of course, sometimes these people will be part of a body that has genuine links with Buddhist organizations in the East and, they would say, are simply continuing practices hallowed by tradition. Others simply have a taste for theatricals.

Does it matter? Is it not really just a matter of taste? Is it not good to keep up these old traditions? Yes, to some extent I'd agree with that. Certainly there is nothing in Buddhism that gives any of us the right to tell others how to live their lives. The old lady who wanted to make people serve apprenticeships was overlooking the fact that absolutely no one has the authority to do that. For that matter, no one has the authority to decide who is a "real" Buddhist and who isn't.

What does bother me is that, if they are to be of any real benefit to us, Buddhism and Zen must become part of *our* culture. The dressing up is all very well for those who have a taste for the exotic, but think of all the people it's putting off. There must be millions of Westerners who would be attracted to Buddhism if they were not discouraged by what looks like mere exhibitionism.

Traditionally Buddhism used to arrive in a new country and quickly melt into the landscape. Chinese Buddhism looks Chinese, Japanese looks Japanese, and so on. Sometimes this melting-in was so complete that outsiders found it hard to recognize the "new" religion. There was a time not so long ago when Tibetan Buddhism was referred to as Lamaism by foreigners and was described as a "degenerate" form of the religion. It turned out that the

very distinctive style of Tibetan Buddhism obscured the fact that it was, in all important respects, still the same religion practiced by the rest of the Buddhist community.

Now we have something different. Instead of westerners taking Buddhism and making it so much a part of their own culture that it melts into the scenery, they keep the exotic trappings and end up with something that looks like a museum exhibit. Think of all the other Eastern imports we now accept without a thought, everything from curry to chess, and tea to karaoke. I think that if, eventually, people decide to let Buddhism become part of our cultural landscape, that could only be a move for the better.

# Zen Inc.

## Toward a modern Zen

In the United States in the 1960s there was a bumper sticker popular with conservative people that said "America—Love It or Leave It!" Those who held more liberal views countered with one that read "America—Change It or Lose It!" The conflict between those who value tradition and those who feel the need for change is as old as human society and occurs all over the world. Zen is now in much the same situation. Buddhists, being a tolerant lot on the whole, don't insult each other with rival bumper stickers but, even so, there are some differences of opinion.

For many people it is important that Zen has been handed down over countless generations. They are aware of the various schools and the lineage by which masters of the past have transmitted Zen through their dharma successors down to the present. The trouble is that the present does not resemble the past one bit. Had Zen stayed in the Far East, in places where its traditions were rooted in home soil, things might have been different. Of course, these modern Eastern societies have also changed drastically, especially since the Second World War, but even so many people there still have a deep understanding and respect for the old ways. Had Zen stayed "at home" there might not have been such an urgent need for it to change. But it didn't. It packed its bags and came West. It landed in societies that were very different from the places where it originated and, amazingly, it took root and grew. Especially, it grew in America, a country that has never been slow to seize upon new ideas and has now probably the largest number of Zen adherents in the world.

The new flowering of Zen is quite miraculous and much to be welcomed. But it is also rather odd. What has happened in many places is that people have tried to re-create traditional Zen in a modern, Western setting.

They've often been to considerable trouble to get it right. Some have gone to Japan and studied long and hard before coming home to teach. They have struggled to make sure that what they bring home with them is authentic Zen.

> To be as effective as it could be, Zen needs to reach more people than just Eastern culture fans.

This is odd because it is rather an un-American thing to do. Imagine that Zen had been a commercial company, Zen Inc. What would have happened? Given the American love of free enterprise and bold corporate drive, it would have found new markets, adapted to local tastes, diversified, and opened franchises in every major city in the country. OK, I know that Zen is different from a corporation, but the principle still applies. To be as effective as it can be, Zen needs to reach more people than just Eastern culture fans and New Age buffs. It needs to blend with the scenery.

Take chess, for example. With its connections to India and China, it has a similar pedigree to Zen. But when you play chess, do you ever think of it as an Oriental game? I doubt it. Chess has become so much a part of Western culture that no one really thinks of it as foreign at all. Zen could do the same. If it does, it may well become a considerable spiritual force in the West. If it doesn't, it will remain a minor curiosity.

# My kind of Zen

## Buddhist compassion versus kindness

All schools of Buddhism put a lot of emphasis on compassion, and Zen is no exception. You regularly hear people talk about feeling (or trying to feel) "compassion for all sentient beings," and Buddhists are always well represented in ecological and animal rights groups. In fact so ingrained is the habit of compassion that you also come across warnings about the dangers of becoming *attached* to compassion. In a world where violence, greed, and selfishness are everyday occurrences, it should be encouraging that at least some people see compassion as a duty. But sometimes I wonder.

It's not that I'm against compassion. Far from it. It's just that I often feel that it is a concept that is just a little too big for humans. Can you honestly say that you feel compassion for, say, the starving people of the Third World? What, *all* of them? Do you *really* feel deeply compassionate toward all the animals that are killed every day to feed a hungry world? I doubt it. I don't for a moment doubt your intentions. I just find it hard to believe that any human mind is actually big enough for the task. Yes, we can feel sorry for the unfortunate. We can feel sympathy when we are shown evidence of suffering in far-flung lands. But, if we are to function at all, we cannot feel constant compassion. At some stage we have to think, "Yes, that's sad, I'll send some money to the appeal fund, but now I'd better get some work done or I'll get fired."

> In pursuit of a big ideal like compassion we can overlook something much more effective that works on a scale we can all understand—kindness.

In pursuit of a big ideal like compassion we can overlook something much more effective that works on a scale we can all understand—kindness. We have all come across people who are so eager to save the world that they rush around doing good, while failing to notice that their kids, their parents, or their friends could use some of their attention. Kindness is not a big idea at all. The good thing about it is that it's tiny and immediate—sort of the spiritual and psychological equivalent of a Kleenex—and even more useful.

Stupidly, we tend to overlook the huge number of chances we get all the time just to be kind to someone. We know we should, but somehow it can get missed in the rush of our lives. This is a pity because we could probably all achieve so much without really investing a huge effort.

I think that those of us who practice Zen really need to keep an eye on this problem. From a certain point of view, Zen is concerned with huge, important issues. Enlightenment, for example. What could possibly be more important than that? After all, it's what all Buddhists are supposed to be aiming for. It is easy to overlook the way that these big issues are inseparable from the small, everyday stuff. But I doubt whether anyone who doesn't really understand the value of simple kindness has much chance of getting to grips with enlightenment.

95

# So, what about the Spanish Inquisition?

Will Zen see me through the rough bits?

When friends discuss my involvement in Zen, there usually comes a moment when they say something like, "But what would you do if you faced the Spanish Inquisition?" OK, this may be an extreme form of the proposition, but it crops up so often in a variety of guises that it's worth an answer.

Having had this conversation a number of times, I now know that it inevitably contains two elements. The first is something like "Would you defend your religion even if it led to your own persecution?" Religious persecution seems to rely on forbidding people from behaving in ways laid down by their religion. My first reaction is that Zen is not like the religions my friends are used to. It has no use for dogma or particular forms of behavior. It doesn't tell me to wear certain clothes, eat or abstain from particular foods, pray a certain number of times a day, or give a percentage of my money to the poor. From the point of view of the casual observer, Zen is invisible, unless I choose to reveal it in some way.

To those who follow Zen, it is more like a journey of exploration than what most people would recognize as religion. Also, the things you discover during this journey are not opinions but the stuff of reality itself. Why would you seek to defend or justify them? It would be a bit like defending the law of gravity. Of course, scientists *have* defended their discoveries against religious bigotry. So why wouldn't Zen do the same? Because, unlike the laws of science, what you discovered through Zen is only available to the discoverer; it can't be given to anyone else.

So is there anything I would be prepared to defend? Yes. I hope I'd have the courage to stand up against cruelty and injustice.

The other element of this discussion usually evolves into a question like, "Will your Zen be strong enough to see you through the rough bits of life?" Here I never hesitate to answer "Yes." I've been lucky that, up to the age of fiftysomething, I've lived a life fairly free of rough bits. Even so, no one gets to middle age without a few problems. I've had to cope with bereavement, career upheaval, relationship problems, and all the other stresses and strains of modern living, and Zen has helped.

The very odd thing about Zen is that even if you give up on it, it never gives up on you. I went through a phase when I worked with a bunch of people who prided themselves on being rational and scientific. The whole ethos of the organization was anti-religious, and, bit by bit, it started to rub off on me. Eventually Zen took a back seat in my life. Then, unexpectedly, the organization was plunged into a difficult period, and for quite a long time my job was in danger. It was a time of great anxiety for me and my family. The funny thing was that I didn't "turn to religion," as many people do when struck down by problems. What happened was that Zen grabbed me fiercely by the scruff of the neck and announced that it was back. What is even odder is that, in the intervening period when I had apparently been doing nothing, my understanding of Zen had deepened considerably.

# Monkey business

## Zen and organized, established religion

Zen has a strong monastic tradition. All the stories you read are about monks, nuns, and homeless mendicants. Even when a layman makes an appearance, he isn't anything like you or me. Take Layman P'ang, for example; he and his daughter heaped all their worldly possessions in a boat, then pushed it into the center of a river and sank it. See what I mean? Not exactly Mr and Miss Average.

One Zen master advised followers to "make poverty your treasure." Buddhism isn't alone in its admiration for poverty. Jesus gave his followers a similar message. All Christians know that you cannot serve God and Mammon, and that a rich man will find it easier to get through the eye of a needle than to enter the kingdom of heaven.

So where does that leave the rest of us? Most people have homes, relationships, kids, jobs, and all the other impedimenta of modern living. Does that mean that we are excluded from Zen? Or, if we continue to take an interest, will it be some sort of degraded second-best Zen that is only a mere shadow of the "real thing?"

I think not. Zen has changed and continues to do so. For a start, it has migrated from the areas where it had its latest flowering and is seeding itself in new places. Also, it is being taken up by new people and adapted to their way of life. This is all to the good. A Zen that is stuck in medieval Japan would be of interest to antiquarians but no one else. However, that does not mean we need to throw out everything to do with the past. The monks of old exhibited qualities of courage and firmness of purpose that we would all do well to emulate. Also their disdain for luxury and worldly comforts has something to say to us when we live in societies where people seldom think of anything else but how to get more of such things.

What is it about poverty that made it so attractive to religious figures of the past? A life without money would lack a lot of the temptations and distractions that might

interrupt religious progress. It would also confer a certain independence on the person who no longer had to sell himself to his employer. But how real are these

**Isn't it better to join the world and find an acceptable way of living in it?**

advantages? Someone said that virtue is merely insufficient temptation. It's easy to be "religious" if you avoid all the things that might bring you face to face with the everyday world. But isn't it better to join that world and find an acceptable way of living in it? Also, isn't the independence of the begging monk an illusion? He is really every bit as dependent as the rest of us, except whereas you may be dependent on General Motors or Microsoft, and I'm dependent on my publishers, the monk depends on the contributions of the faithful. It's said that, because those contributions are made as an act of piety, that makes it OK. But that's a thin excuse. When you accept money from someone, you are giving them a piece of your independence, even if you're wearing a monk's robe.

The monastic tradition has served Zen well and should certainly not be despised. But it is clearly not the way of the future. We will find our own way, one that helps us live in our own society in a way that fits in with our own needs. And it will be a good way.

# People of the book

## Buddhist scriptures

Muslims sometimes refer to themselves, Jews, and Christians as the "People of the Book," meaning that they all have a common biblical background. However much the three religions may disagree, at least they always have things in common to disagree about. Buddhism has no Bible. There are, to be sure, some very important scriptures that Buddhists would agree are central to their beliefs, but no one book that says it all. Also, because Buddhism does not claim to be divinely inspired, there are no writings that are regarded as holy writ and are therefore beyond criticism.

It comes as a bit of a shock to outsiders to realise that Buddhism has no real equivalent of the Ten Commandments. There are the Five Precepts, of course. But what is a precept? It's really no more than a guide, a bit of good advice. Christians sometimes point out that, unlike the Commandments, the precepts are all negative. To an extent they are right; the precepts tell you the sort of things you shouldn't do. What they fail to understand is that we also have the Noble Eightfold Path, that tells you all the things you *should* do. But once again, it boils down to good advice, not instructions from above.

Buddhism has an enviably large number of scriptures, not to mention commentaries beyond counting. This approach has had its advantages. Although people can and do quarrel about the precise meaning of one passage or another, no one is tempted to go to war in order to wipe out the heretical views of others. You might think, assuming that you have been brought up in the monotheistic tradition of the Big Three religions, that this multiplicity of scriptures would lead to a mishmash of views in which anyone could believe just about anything they liked. In theory this is so, though in practice it seems that Buddhists share a high degree of agreement on most issues.

The main difference between Buddhism and the Big Three religions is that Buddhists are making a journey entirely of their own volition, without prompting from any god. The longer you go on, the more it seems like an exploration that you undertake out of intense curiosity rather than something that you do from a sense of moral duty. No one ever says, "Do this and do not do that. Or else."

> Each [story] contains a tiny nugget of Zen that will, if you let it, expand and enrich your understanding.

They may say, "If you do this you'll end up regretting it," but that's different.

Zen is particularly quirky on the subject of scriptures. They are seen as no more than a useful prop, something to help you on your road to understanding, but of no permanent value. Once they have served their purpose they can be tossed aside. Zen also makes extensive use of stories. These are not really scriptures at all, but traditional tales of the doings of Zen masters and students. The closest Christian equivalent would be the parables of Jesus, though Zen stories are more than parables. They often do make a moral point, but that is seldom, if ever, the whole point of the story. Each one contains a tiny nugget of Zen that will, if you let it, expand and enrich your understanding. Like all stories, they circulate by word of mouth, in books, magazines, and, these days, on the Internet. And though there are venerable and authoritative translations, there is no Authorized Version. These are folk tales and are told as such. They are one of the great treasures of Zen and worth more than a whole libraryful of books.

# Whatever turns you on

Buddhism and tolerance

Some people say, "If you've got it, flaunt it."
What Buddhism has to flaunt is an
abundance of tolerance. It isn't spiritually cool
to make unflattering comparisons with other
religions, so I won't. But the tolerance of Buddhism is very
interesting and I've often wondered where it comes from.

If you look at the teachings of the world's major
religions, there is much that urges people to live in peace
with others, regardless of their beliefs. Sometimes people
listened. Although no major religious leader said, "Go out
and massacre everyone who disagrees with you," that was
all too often the message that got through. Why didn't
that happen in Buddhism? If you look at Buddhist history
you will find plenty of disagreements, even arguments and
hard words over points of doctrine. But no bloodshed.
These days the various sects live together in increasingly
close harmony. This very welcome development has come
about because of the naïve enthusiasm of hordes of

Westerners who dash back and forth
between one sect and another spreading
goodwill as they go.

Probably the greatest advantage
Buddhism possessed was the absence of a
god. Buddha was a man, though a remark-
able one. His teachings, uniquely among
religious leaders, are noted for their lack of
bossiness. You are guided and advised rather
than ordered about. Amazingly, this tradition
has survived. Although Buddhist monks may
have a difficult time with teachers who drive
them hard on the path to enlightenment, for
laypeople the religion is easy-going. It isn't
a case of "anything goes"—the standards aimed at are as
high as those of any other religion—but there is a sense
that you won't improve people by nagging or bullying.
Instead, you have to encourage them to find the right way
for themselves. Buddhism is always about education rather
than punishment.

The other major Buddhist asset is the lack of a divinely
inspired Bible. We have more scriptures than you can
shake a stick at. There's plenty of room for argument but,
since none of the scriptures claims divine origin, no one
feels obliged to defend their view to the death. That
doesn't mean that Buddhists never entertain intolerant
thoughts. It's just that it is very, very tough to find any way
of justifying them. Somehow, when you lack a book of

words that you can twist to mean what you want, it is harder to ignore the original message. Even though Buddha's words are not reliably recorded, his message comes through loud and clear, even when it's inconvenient.

Sadly, this excess of tolerance is hard to export. Want to try telling the Christians, Jews, and Muslims how much better off they'd be without God or scriptures? Hmmm. Maybe not. It would be seen as impertinence to suggest that Buddhism has The Answer (implying that the other religions don't.) So what do we do? Hug ourselves that we have such a groovy religion and leave everyone else to their schisms and persecutions? No. Buddhism is clear on the idea of sharing the good things you have with others. Perhaps the way Buddhists can express gratitude for tolerance is to join those people brave enough to stand up for tolerance against bigotry, discrimination, and persecution. This would be neither easy nor comfortable (which is one way you know that it's probably the right thing to do). If you've got it, flaunt it. But tolerance isn't a Ferrari or a holiday home in Florida. The only real way to flaunt it is to use it, however uncomfortable that may be.

# Buddha, can you spare a dime?

## Why are there no Zen charities?

Walk down any main street in a Christian country and you'll see someone rattling a charity box at you and, very frequently, the charity they're collecting for will be a Christian organization. Judaism is also renowned for its charitable works and Islam also makes charity a duty for its followers. So what about Buddhists? Have you ever seen the Red Wheel (as opposed to the Red Cross)? Have you ever been to a Buddhist country and had a collecting box rattled under your nose by someone collecting for a Buddhist charity that sends aid to the starving? The answer is almost certainly "no." Why not? Are Buddhists mean? Don't they care about others? The answer is complicated but interesting.

First, you have to understand that Buddhist countries mostly work on the principle of the extended family. This is quite a different concept from our Western idea of family, which, at best, extends beyond our immediate circle only as far as a few half-forgotten cousins. A true extended family takes in all sorts of people who have a claim of kinship. Some of these families can be enormous, and the only Western organization I've come across that is similar in size and purpose is the Scottish clan. An individual's relationship to other members of the family is not just a matter of sentiment (which often plays a very small part) but is usually extremely practical and involves supplying money, work, accommodation, and food. In countries where there are often only the most rudimentary public services, this sort of self-help society is vital.

Once you find yourself chipping in regularly to help out members of your family, your attitude to complete strangers changes for the worse.

Also, Buddhists perform charitable acts by supporting the *sangha* or community of monks. Giving donations of food and money to the monks is considered very important and, if you get up early enough, you will often see a line of monks going from door to door accepting donations from the faithful. This has a double benefit because the monks don't keep everything they are given for themselves. Some of it they pass on to the waifs and strays who arrive at their temple begging for help. They often even support stray animals that turn up looking for shelter and, according to Buddhist custom, cannot be turned away.

The really important difference between the Buddhist way and those of other religions is that, for Buddhists, the concept of doing something for others is alien. This is not hard-heartedness, it is just that it is a very important point in Buddhism that there *are* no others. Everything is joined together, everyone is a part of everyone else. To Westerners this can sound like a cop-out. Maybe for some people it is. But for those who take Buddhism seriously this is a very important point. Your existence cannot be seen as separate from the existences of other creatures (not just people.) Everything you do affects everybody. Therefore the Western practice of rushing about doing good to "others" is replaced by a more gentle process in which believers try to use their influence to improve the whole of life around them.

# No sex, please, we're Buddhists

## Zen, Buddhism and sex

It's a little discouraging to realize that whereas in so many ways Buddhism is refreshingly different from other religions, when it comes to sex it's depressingly similar. Zen, which I would have hoped would be the honorable exception, is no different than any other Buddhist school in this respect.

Just about any religion you can think of has a problem with sex or, at least, sex that's (shudders of horror) fun. Naturally, procreation has to be allowed or religions would pretty soon run out of adherents, but, as any married couple can tell you, there's a world of difference between procreation and real, rollicking, rolling-in-the-hay sex. We're told that sex as an expression of our love for each other is OK, but anything else is lust, and lust is *out*.

This all seems very odd. Any observer of the human species can't fail to notice that sex is one of the major forces that drives us. It operates both openly and

117

clandestinely in all sorts of ways. It permeates the whole fabric of our lives. Quite often matters that appear to have nothing to do with sex are in fact being affected by it. For example, people who are attracted to each other (but have no intention of sleeping together) might easily become allies in other ways, such as in a business relationship.

Why does religion try so hard (and with a complete lack of success) to marginalize such a powerful force? One answer might be that sex is so powerful that it can easily distract us from the less obvious charms of religion. The love of God, apparently infinite and all-encompassing, can, from an all too human point of view, seem less desirable than the love of Sam, Rosie, Ted, or Alice. Maybe religions just get jealous.

Buddhism has another answer and it's to do with attachment. As I have said elsewhere in this book, being "attached" is a major no-no for Buddhists (see pages 33–35.) The aim is to liberate oneself from attachments. Of course, this runs you straight into a brick wall because, if sex is an attachment, then so is love, even the supposedly "safe," allowable, married variety.

Buddhism sprang from a monastic tradition and for centuries has been associated with monkish behavior. It is easy to see how a bunch of single-sex religious adherents living in a closed community might find sex a problem. There is even a Theravadin meditative practice in which you are supposed to sit and contemplate the hideousness of the body. You think about hair and how repulsive it is,

about skin and how it oozes with sweat, and so on. To me, however, this all sounds a bit neurotic.

It is interesting, however, that the monks were not quite consistent in their quest for non-attachment. There are many examples of Zen masters rhapsodizing over the wonders of nature. The beauty of the moon, the breath-taking views from a mountain, the grace of a bamboo grove—these have all formed the basis for Zen poetry. Why not a beautiful girl (or boy) with no clothes on?

Zen is about life. All of it. It's not some cosy little game to be played out in a temple. Sex is such a major part of life that only a fool would try to ignore it. While it might not be easy, unless your Zen can cope with sex maybe it isn't really Zen at all.

# Surrender your ego (to mine!)

## Letting go of yourself—carefully

Many religions regard the ego as a Bad Thing. It gets blamed for being that nasty, self-seeking bit of us that not only makes us less responsive to the needs and feelings of others, but also confines us to the realms of "I want" when we could be contemplating more spiritual matters. Buddhism is particularly insistent on freeing us from the illusion of our limited ego-selves and opening us up to the big picture. All this is fine in theory, but, in practice, trying to achieve this egoless state often raises more problems than it solves.

Humility is usually advertised as being the gateway to greater spiritual development. You should, we are told, rigorously suppress your own thoughts, desires, opinions, and beliefs. By surrendering your ego in this way, you will be better able to grow in spiritual stature. Monks and nuns, both Christian and Buddhist, have always fought tirelessly to achieve this state of humility and root out the malicious workings of the ego.

I see two problems with this, and they both bother me quite a lot. The first is that simply by concentrating so hard on your ego, you are in fact lending it strength. It's a bit like someone who's giving up smoking, alcohol, or drugs. The more you struggle not to give in to your bad habit, the more you really, really want to. Some people may achieve a state where they have finally outgrown the habit and left it behind for ever. But many more settle for living in a state of constant armed resistance. This is not an ego-less state, and someone who is constantly obsessed with maintaining a sort of false humility is, arguably, worse off than someone who never made the effort in the first place.

Secondly, if I give up my own desires, opinions, and so on, what do I put in their place? The short answer is someone else's. People have a rather romantic, misty-eyed notion that Zen is full of wise old masters who are just waiting to guide you to enlightenment. In fact, though there may be some people of great wisdom, you don't get many of them to the pound. Most of the people you come across will be perfectly ordinary mortals just like yourself. They may have some experience of Zen and they might well be able to teach you, but that is not really a good enough reason to turn yourself over to them entirely. Many people simply cannot

122

resist the idea of being the boss of something or other. Being the boss of a "religious" group actually gives you more power over willing victims than being the boss in, say, an office. It is therefore quite normal to come across people who are far more interested in maintaining their control over a group than they are in the spiritual development of the people within the group.

Where does this leave us? First, if your ego is illusory, and I believe that it is, then the best thing to do is observe it carefully (as you do through zazen) but otherwise leave it alone. Don't lend it strength by struggling against it, just let it unravel from want of attention. Second, by all means be guided by people who have more experience than you do, but don't be in too much of a hurry to believe that they are to be obeyed without question. As we have already learned, Buddha was clear that teachers, including himself, should be open to question.

# Zen is what you are, not what you believe

## How you live is more important than doctrine

When friends introduce me to new acquaintances, having given them all the usual biographical stuff, they tend to add, by way of an extra attraction, "He believes in Zen." Strictly speaking it isn't true but, for the sake of a quiet life, I usually let it slide. The truth is that I *used* to believe in Zen once, when I was young and didn't know any better. I bought books on Buddhism, joined the Cambridge University Buddhist Society (whose lectures I attended zealously,) and engaged in discussions with every passing monk I could reasonably waylay. I carefully memorized all the things I was supposed to believe and put a lot of mental effort into making sure I thought all the right thoughts. The trouble is, Zen isn't like that.

125

As my practice of zazen progressed I found that everything was quite different to the way I had imagined it would be. It made absolutely no difference what I believed or what I thought. Once you start to meditate, Zen works within you, like it or not. You have about as much influence over it as you do over the way your hair grows. This can be slightly disconcerting. You may have imagined that you were making moral choices and following doctrines laid down centuries ago by wise masters, whereas you only made one choice, to practice Zen (there is even a lingering suspicion that this choice may not have been entirely your own either.)

When your practice matures, you find that Zen is no longer something separate, something that has been stuck on like a mask. It *is* you. The Zen master Shunryu Suzuki said that it was like walking through the rain and slowly getting soaked through. That's a very nice analogy. You don't notice on a day-by-day basis that your Zen practice is maturing but, over time, you see the improvement in yourself. Other people begin to notice it too, though they might not be able to pin down just how you've changed. Zen is best known for the violent, spectacular experience of *satori*, or enlightenment, but for most people, most of the time it's a much gentler process of growth and maturity.

Eventually Zen is so much a part of your life that you no longer have a separate name for it. To give it any name at all seems pointless. It's rather like being a fish in a pond. The water of Zen is within you and without you and *is* you.

Can you separate the fish from the water? Well, you could, but then you'd have a dead fish. So in an important way the water *is* the fish. Does a fish believe in water? No, it doesn't need to. The water is an essential part of its being, from which it is inseparable. Do you believe in Zen? Eventually you no longer give it a thought. Am I being mindful? Am I cultivating non-attachment? Am I keeping the precepts? Whereas you once had to carry these questions about with you like so much heavy luggage, eventually your Zen is able to cope without them. You no longer believe in Zen, it's just what you are.

# Losing my religion

## How Zen drives out "religion"

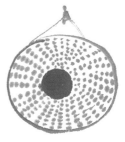

I used to organize a regular conference at Cambridge University's Magdalene College (it's pronounced "maudlin"—don't ask.) One of the highlights was always a debate, and one year I decided to let them loose on the perennially popular God question. What amazed and horrified me was when they were given the chance to discuss God, all these very bright people could do was squabble about the version of God that their parents and teachers had given them when they were very small. Psychologically, seeing all that regression in one place was fascinating, though religiously, it was very depressing. It made me see why religion, and the rejection of religion, have caused so many of the world's problems. Many of these people seemed still to believe in some sort of kindly-old-man-on-a-cloud God, while others were busy rejecting God-the-very-cruel-king-who's-just-like-my-father. My own religious experience had been very different.

I went through a Buddhist phase where I did all the right stuff—made Buddha shrines, lit incense sticks and candles, read scriptures, talked to learned monks, the whole bit. Then I went through a Zen phase where I did other right-on stuff, such as wrestling with koans and devoting myself to zazen. Now I don't do any of that. You can scour our house for Buddha images and come up with only a couple of ornaments, which are neither displayed above head height nor given offerings of incense, etc. My wife, who never had much enthusiasm for Buddhism (or any other religion) secretly hopes that I've grown out of the whole thing. But she's wrong. It's more that I've grown *into* it.

Once you start compartmentalizing your life, you lose the plot. If there is a compartment called "religion" that is separate from other compartments called things like "work," "home," "family," and "friends," then you really have a problem. On the other hand, I'm not crazy about religions that thrust themselves into every corner of people's lives. It is possible to do this in Zen if you want to. There are prayers for absolutely everything, including a couple of hilarious ones for relieving yourself and brushing your teeth. This isn't what I mean by religion pervading your whole life. This is just a slightly bullying, officious form of religion that is strutting about making a nuisance of itself.

In Zen, once you reach a certain level of understanding, the forms and rituals of religion are no longer relevant. Life is just all one, whether you're working in your office, or playing ball with the kids, or trying to fix the car's engine. It's rather like the way we give the oceans different names. Are they really different? No, of course not; they're all just one great body of water. The divisions make it easier for us to think about them in a certain way, but they all hide from us the fact that all that water is actually just one big ocean. Religion hides from us the fact that all life is just *life*, and we don't need to fuss over it.

> Life is just all one, whether you're working in your office, or playing ball with the kids, or trying to fix the car's engine.

131

# Instant Zen: just add hot water

## The quest for immediate spiritual gratification

We live in an age of instant gratification. If we want something we want it now. If we are fortunate enough to live in
one of the prosperous parts of the world we can usually
have our wish. Communications have been so speeded up
by cell phones, email, and the Internet that we can get
what we want, even if it comes from a great distance, in
next to no time. The ubiquitous credit card ensures that we
can have our heart's desire even when we don't have the
money to pay for it. Where our parents would have saved
up the cash, we flash the plastic.

The trouble is that not everything is for sale in quite
that way. Spiritual progress is slow, painstaking, and
thoroughly unmodern. You can't even hurry it, let alone buy
it. That can cause huge frustrations. I once gave a seminar
on Zen to a small group gathered in a suburban house.
I talked for a while and gave them an introduction, then led
them in their first period of zazen. I knew that they were all
complete novices so I kept the session short. I wasn't

133

particularly surprised that
they found it hard to sit for thirty
minutes, but I was astonished afterward
that they clearly felt disappointed that
"nothing had happened." What did they expect?
If you learn a language, or how to play a musical
instrument, do you expect to achieve expertise after your
first lesson? Of course not. So why should Zen be different?

Even so, many people do feel that they want spiritual
experience to be available on tap. This makes them
vulnerable to every cheat, swindler, and phoney-baloney
religious adept in town. There is no shortage whatever of
people who promise instant results. Unfortunately it is not
hard to produce a few cheap, "spiritual" tricks that will
impress the gullible. Some people are so eager to believe

(something, *anything*) that they are easy meat for the unscrupulous. What is even sadder is that some people end up rushing from one spiritual practice to another without ever finding what they seek. Individually, some of these practices might have value but, because they are given no time to work, our eager seeker after enlightenment is soon dashing off to investigate something new.

The truth about Zen is that it does not come in a pot to which you can add hot water and leave for two minutes. Also, it is not an emergency measure that you can resort to when your life starts to go wrong. Zen needs lots and lots of time to develop. You build up understanding over years and you never stop growing. What you thought you understood last year will be obsolete this year and laughably naïve by next year. The upside is that, if you take time and trouble over your Zen, it will prove a steadfast friend, and though it won't prevent you from hitting rough patches in your life (nothing will,) it will certainly enable you to deal with them and come out stronger and wiser.

# Time, time, time

## The benefits of aging

Human beings are almost unique in the natural world because they live to a great age. Most creatures die before even attaining sexual maturity. We not only go on to complete our biological mission (to breed and raise children), but we also often live on into old age, and, increasingly, that time of our lives is seen as a productive one.

When I was teaching in Thailand I came across a novel concept. People believed that wisdom increased with age. Older people were not only listened to and respected, but were actively sought out and asked for their advice. Of course I had heard of such a thing before. Literature is full of references to elderly people of great wisdom. In modern Western countries, however, it is an idea that is out of favor. Youth is in, age is out. The young are seen as enthusiastic, creative, unprejudiced, and fashionable. They are frequently some or all of these things and it is right that we should value them. What they don't have is experience. The only way to get that is to live a long time. Even then experience can't be taken for granted. You have to want to grow in wisdom. Some people don't. Some get stuck early on and never change their opinions again for as long as they live. This is rather sad for them.

Many young people find Zen attractive because it seems fresh, unstuffy, and not overburdened by the trappings of formal religion. Also, they like the idea of an enlightenment that can strike like lightning at any moment. That's all fine. Except that usually enlightenment doesn't strike as quickly as people would like. In fact, one of the things that is special about Zen is that, as you progress, you come to a very different understanding of what enlightenment actually is. You have to be prepared for a long slog to find out what Zen is really all about.

Soto Zen, the variety that is most frequently found in the West, puts great emphasis on the gradual ripening of understanding. It is sometimes likened to the ripening of fruit that, when ready, will drop from the tree without encouragement. As I get older I notice that I'm developing qualities of tolerance and good temper that, in spite of all my best efforts and my Zen practice, were sadly lacking when I was younger.

Similarly, other responses are modified by age. When I was young the sight of a pretty girl set off a flood of hormones, with predictable results. You can make some pretty disastrous mistakes that way and, believe me, if there were mistakes to be made I made my full share. Now I'm older it's much easier to treat people as people and see past any initial attraction to what lies below.

This also works in reverse. I used to dislike people for trifling reasons and allow slights and insults to rankle with me. Now it's much easier to be tolerant and forgiving. It's not that I never get angry, but it happens less often and it's much easier to let go of the anger when it arises.

It's good that young people find that Zen offers them the spiritual path they need, and it's even better when they find out that it still has plenty to offer when the first flush of youth is over.

There are other advantages. Traditionally, the words of Zen masters were confusing and hard to fathom. Yet as I grow older I find myself more and more often thinking, "Ah, so *that's* what he meant."

# What do we tell the children?

## Buddhism for the pre-teen set

I was on a Zen email list when a lady started a
correspondence about how she should educate
her children to be Buddhists. It was an interesting
problem. First, there is not much written that's suitable
for children. Also, it seems that though there are plenty of
Buddhist centers around, they don't generally cater for
children. Just out of interest I phoned our local one and
asked the question. The answer was more "Um" than Om.

Educating children in an "unusual" religion is bound to
give them some problems. Standing out from the crowd is
not a highly desirable quality for many youngsters. So
maybe the first thing we need to get clear is why we
would want to educate our children in this way. If it's just
because we want them to be like us and toe the family
line, perhaps that isn't a good enough reason. Probably
most Buddhists would say that they
think their religion has the most
satisfactory system for living

that they have found, and that they would like their children to enjoy it too. After all, almost no Western adults have themselves been brought up as Buddhists; they have come to it through personal exploration. That seems like a pretty good aim, but how do you go about achieving it?

I've never felt that handing my kids great dollops of Eastern thought was going to do anything but put them off. They already look askance at people who are into what they describe as "sad old hippy stuff."

> Teaching by example is hard work. It keeps you on your toes and you sometimes make a mess of it. But I think it's the best form of religious education you can give.

I have, as a matter of general knowledge, told them some of the background to Buddhism, but I have never tried to get them to memorize any of it. That doesn't mean they get away without religious education. Like all teenagers, they ask questions, and my answers are inevitably colored by my beliefs. Just because I don't preface every remark with, "As the Zen master so-and-so tells us. . ." doesn't mean that the thoughts aren't Zen thoughts.

The best way to teach anyone anything is by example. I'd much rather that in the future my kids thought, "Dad did it that way and it worked for him," than that they remembered some quotation from a Zen scripture. Teaching by example is hard work. It keeps you on your toes and you sometimes make a mess of it. But I think it's the best form of religious education you can give.

# I wanna live forever

## But would it be a good idea?

This bottle of potion I have on my desk is for you. I'm giving it to you free of charge. All you have to do is ask. Don't look so suspicious—it tastes of nothing worse than banana milkshake. What does it do? Simple. It confers eternal youth. And, just to show that I really care, you can have beauty and wealth at no extra charge. Not a bad deal when you consider what you paid for the book. So— do you want it? Ah, not so fast. Before you knock it back in one gulp, have you thought this through?

Mostly we regard age and death with abhorrence. We manage not to think or talk about them too much, or we disguise what we really feel under a handy blanket of euphemism. The old first became "Senior Citizens" and then they were said to be "enjoying their Golden Years." Death is a subject we really try to steer clear of because, let's face it, on any list of "100 Things to do on a Wet Afternoon," dying wouldn't even score. So, just like the Kids from Fame, you wanna live forever?

I once wrote a story about someone who discovered the secret of eternal youth. It started out as a bit of light-hearted science fiction but soon I found the tone getting darker. If you live forever, you lose everybody else. How can you have relationships with people who are suddenly so ephemeral? They drift past you like ships on their way to the breaker's yard, while you sail on, unaffected by time. My hero was forced to abandon each new wife on her thirtieth birthday and wander off in search of a new life. Effectively he became detached from those around him and, of course, because he no longer fully shared their humanity, he started to treat people as things to be used for his own convenience. It was a dark tale.

Suppose that we *all* had eternal youth. What then? Wouldn't that sort out the problem? No, because a death-less society would be a completely stagnant one. If no one died, there'd be no room for anyone to be born. We'd have to stop having children. And, let's face it, we'd get bored. Life can be wonderful, fascinating, full of joy and adventure, but for*ever?* No—after the first hundred or so years it might begin to pall just a little. After a few hundred you'd be desperate to die.

The Christian burial service says, "In the midst of life we are in death." But that's not quite it. Life and death aren't different. And you certainly can't say Life is Good, Death is Bad, because they are actually the same. Life is wonderful because it is fragile, transient, and there is a sweet sadness about the inevitability of our parting.

When I was in Thailand, I missed the beautiful colors of the fall. Thailand has its seasons, of course, but they are all so lively. The heat is followed by rain and the so-called cool season would rank as a hot English summer. At no time is there that gentle, melancholy period that marks the end of one year and the start of the next. So, though I'm not in a hurry to die, I'm quite sure that without death I cannot truly live.

Life is wonderful because it
is fragile, transient, and there
is a sweet sadness about the
inevitability of our parting.

# Born-again Zen

## The doctrine of rebirth

During the coffee break at a conference, a
lady was busy telling us how she'd become a
born-again Christian when another new
acquaintance chipped in, "I suppose that
makes me a born-again, and again, and again Buddhist."
Rebirth is one feature of Buddhism that fascinates people,
though, strangely, it is not much mentioned in Zen.

To me, the jury is still out on rebirth. It's one of those
areas where I take full advantage of the Buddha's advice
to find out for yourself. I have never seen the slightest
evidence to suggest that people are reborn. But there are
things that make me take the idea seriously. First, there's
karma. I *know* that karma works (see pages 49–51) in daily
life. It isn't an opinion, it's a fact. I've seen it in operation
in my own life and those of others. The trouble is that, if
we cease to exist at death, the story is left unfinished.
Now life isn't a work of fiction and there is nothing to say
that the end should be neat and tidy, but when someone
has clearly been going through a process of learning, of
striving toward a deeper understanding, it seems

unsatisfactory that it should be brought to a sudden halt. I don't like to see education wasted.

Then there are the odd things that happen. There are people who remember previous lives. Are they just eccentric or deranged? Quite possibly, but maybe not. But what is more interesting is the way children arrive in this world apparently having knowledge and interests that they could not have picked up during this life. My daughter developed a precocious interest in Native Americans. This is much odder than it sounds. First, the days of Westerns on TV are long over in the UK. When I was a kid in the 1950s, we all knew an Apache from a Cheyenne, and remembered what happened to General Custer. Thanks to TV, many British kids knew more about the history and geography of the United States than they did about their own country. But to my daughter's generation, all that is a closed book. Yet she arrived thirsty for knowledge on the topic. So where did she get her interest from?

> Zen teaches you how to live in this moment. If you want philosophical speculation on life and death, you're in the wrong place.

Another strange thing has caught my attention. It's the way some old people start to talk about what they'll do "next time." My mother says it from time to time. She isn't a believer in rebirth. She's a sort of wishy-washy Christian but, nevertheless, from time to time she makes a few plans for "next time." Some of these are humorous ("Next time, I'll have the sense to be born a man,") but others sound like she means them.

None of this counts as anything like proof and, as I say, the jury is out. And it really doesn't matter. Zen doesn't bother much about the afterlife. Imagine that you're a chunk of ice floating in the ocean. The waters warm and you melt. Did you die? Will you be reborn? Is it worth a moment's thought? Zen teaches you how to live in this moment. If you want philosophical speculation on life and death, you're in the wrong place.

# We're all going to Graceland

## Faith, works, and grace in Zen

My first experience of Buddhism was with the Theravadin
School in Thailand. Theravadins believe that if you do
enough good deeds you will store up so much "merit" that,
eventually, you will gain entry to nirvana. Privately I used
to think of merit rather disparagingly as "Brownie points."
My head, and even my heart, may have been Buddhist, but
my feet were still firmly planted in the rocky soil of my
Scottish childhood, and every wee Calvinist knows that
you don't get to heaven through Good Works, or even
through Faith, but only by the Grace of God. Grace was a
very interesting concept. You couldn't do anything to get
it. You *certainly*, as a mere sinner, could never deserve it.
But, for some people, it just happened. Its workings were
unpredictable and depended entirely on the unfathomable
Will of God.

As it has no god, Buddhism is immune to the workings of Grace but, years later when I discovered Zen,
I realized that this idea of something incomprehensible

153

that strikes out of a clear blue sky was not a purely Scottish invention.

Zen is big on the idea of lightning striking. Read a collection of Zen stories and you will come across any number of accounts of people who were suddenly and inexplicably enlightened. Of course, most of these people had been searching hard for enlightenment and, even though good deeds aren't enough to buy your way in, these people would probably have also performed such deeds in abundance. But what really fascinated me were the occasional stories of people who received this lightning bolt of insight when they were not even hoping for it.

Zen is unpredictable and apparently capricious. In this way it has much in common with the concept of Grace I understood as a child. Naturally, most people who go in search of it will conform to the normal profile of religious people everywhere. They will pray, meditate, perform good deeds, and study the scriptures. But, at the end of the day, lightning will strike where it wants to and not, however much we want and encourage it to, where it is not yet ready to strike.

This can, of course, be discouraging. You read again and again of people who have almost beaten their brains out trying to get enlightened, only to be disappointed. Sometimes they give up and then, in the very act of giving up, they receive the illumination that has eluded them. Because the huge double-bind of Zen is that, on the one hand, we are told that you must want enlightenment as

much as a man whose head is held under water wants air, on the other hand wanting it so urgently is a form of attachment and a hindrance to achieving your goal. In fact even thinking of enlightenment as a "goal" is a good way of making sure you don't get it.

I used to find this awfully discouraging. It made the idea of Catch 22 seem almost cosy. Later on I started to see the sense of it. Zen has a sort of unintentionality that creeps up on you. Just as beginning swimmers sink because they struggle too hard, Zen learners want too much. Zen comes when it comes. It takes patience—and Grace.

# Why are you telling me this?

## Self-help Zen

The idea of writing a book full of good advice worries me. First, people seldom want advice and, second, what makes me think I'm qualified to give it? My normal rule is that I don't offer an opinion unless it's asked for. You handed over your hard-earned cash for this book so I guess that's let me off the hook. You asked. But what about my qualifications?

Traditionally a Zen student would go through a long and tough apprenticeship before his master would give him his seal of approval and let him loose to teach others. Nowadays, for good or ill, Zen has been democratized. All you need to become an "expert" on Zen is to buy a couple of paperbacks. There are plenty of people about who can walk the walk and talk the talk. There is also no shortage of people who fancy themselves as religious teachers with disciples to hang on their words of wisdom.

The upside of the way Zen has developed is that it has become much easier for people to help each other. Thanks to modern communications it's simple to keep in touch with other students throughout the world. I sometimes think it's a little like a bunch of people climbing a mountain together. Every now and then someone shouts out to those below, "Look out for that big rock on the left, it's slippery as hell!" Two minutes later, someone yells, "There's a great handhold just here!" Maybe the old Zen masters would have disapproved. But it's the way things are. Zen masters are few and far between, but Zen students are plentiful. Self-help seems the only way forward.

I found Zen over twenty-five years ago and knew immediately that it was what I'd been looking for. I have no idea why. I'd been attracted to the Far East since I was a child and, when I came across Buddhism it was like meeting an old friend I'd lost touch with. When I came across Zen the sense of belonging was even more intense.

During my adult years I've worked to understand Zen and make it the center of my life. That does not make me some sort of saint. I've done plenty of stupid, thoughtless, and unkind things in my time. But I've never stopped trying to make things better. Zen is not about being perfect. It's about being human and struggling to come to terms with that humanity. That's what I've done and, if my experience is of any value to you, then I offer it gladly.

Zen is not about being perfect.
It's about being human and
struggling to come to terms
with that humanity.
That's what I've done and, if
my experience is of any value
to you, then I offer it gladly.

This edition published by the Michael Friedman
Publishing Group, Inc. by arrangement with MQ
Publications Limited.

ISBN 1-58663-711-8

2002 Friedman/Fairfax
© 2002 MQ Publications Limited
Text © 2002 Robert Allen

1 3 5 7 9 10 8 6 4 2

For bulk purchases and special sales, please
contact:

Michael Friedman Publishing Group, Inc.
Attention: Sales Department
230 Fifth Avenue, Suite 700
New York, NY 10001
212 / 685-6610 FAX 2123 / 685-3916

Visit our website:
www.metrobooks.com